Wake Up!

AN AWAKENING OF PURPOSE

By

Jermaine C. Holland

© Copyright 2019 by Jermaine C. Holland - All rights reserved.

It is not legal to reproduce, duplicate, or transmit any part of this document in either electronic means or printed format. Recording of this publication is strictly prohibited.

This book is dedicated to my beautiful children, Cristopher, Joshua, and Jaya.

Love always,
Dad

Table of Contents

Introduction 1

Chapter One: The Awakening 2

Chapter Two: The Law of Immunity 4

Chapter Three: Heal and Deal 7

Chapter Four: Spiritual Maintenance 17

Chapter Five: Finding the Real Me 20

Chapter Six: The Mind Game 23

Chapter Seven: Love and Passions 27

Awakening Exercises 1-5 31

Bibliography 39

Acknowledgments 40

About the Author 41

Introduction

Growing up as a pastor's kid or "PK" as we affectionately call it, I saw life from one perspective. At times, something on the inside of me felt like life should different. I would often hear pastors preach or speakers teaching about finding and walking in your purpose, but it never really clicked for me. I went through years of my life going through the motion. This led to me feeling drained from life itself. Then, after going through my own process, God came and gave me a burst of life. An awakening! The irony is, I never even knew I was sleep. There were so many things that happened over time that caused me to become this person I couldn't recognize. This person didn't match who I thought I really was and who I would eventually become.

As you read this book, keep in mind that I am not a clinical therapist, spiritual advisor, or licensed counselor of any kind. I am however, a supporter of seeking professional mental health services and I encourage you to do so. This book is simply a short read of ideas, concepts and principles that have helped me reach a level of awareness and activation, if you will. This book acts as a defibrillator that will shock your inner man into awareness of purpose! You don't have a choice not to be who you are purposed to be in this life. The alarm has sounded. It's time to WAKE UP!

Chapter One: The Awakening

Often times, God puts us in uncomfortable situations so that we will use the frustration and irritation to move, wake up, and realize that we have been barely moving through life in a sleeping state. While in this state, you eventually realize that what you have been doing hasn't been working. You may begin to experience deeper feelings that there is more to life and more for you. This is the place where you are sick and tired of being sick and tired. You are tired of trying to figure it out. Yes, that place! It is in that place in our lives when we are "awakened".

Have you ever looked around and thought to yourself, I've done so much work, yet I have nothing to show for it? Or perhaps you've thought, I love my spouse or partner and they love me, but something is still missing. Do you want to be happy for others yet you find yourself secretly picking them apart because of your own insecurities? As hard as they are, these are the types of tough questions you will have to begin to ask yourself if you REALLY want to breakthrough into purposeful living. You have to get so tired of not bearing fruit and so hungry to prosper! The fact is you deserve to prosper but there's one thing stopping you…PURPOSE. As much as we may try to avoid or ignore it, there is no way we can get around it. God put us on this earth as an agent with a specific purpose. As an agent for God, you must accept and complete missions in HIS name and in HIS honor. After all, he died so we may live!

Here's a little something you may not know about me. I love expensive, designer, handcrafted shoes! For the sake of explaining this concept, let's say I purchase a pair of these designer shoes. I mean these shoes are the most sought after and the best shoe ever made. Imagine me getting home with my new designer shoes to only find out, they don't fit. Now, because I'm such a shoe lover I could keep the shoes at home on display and just admire how beautiful and uniquely crafted they are. I could even return them and get my money back or better yet give them away to someone who could fit them. The point is no matter how much money I paid for these shoes, they would not serve their intended purpose for me, which is to wear them. Not serving your intended purpose is never a good thing. You don't want to be that ill fit pair of expensive designer shoes to God. You want to operate in your purpose. It's time to get up from sleeping and awaken your spirit to everything within you!

Chapter Two: The Law of Immunity

Merriam-Webster Dictionary defines the word *immune* as being free, exempt; marked by protection; not susceptible or responsive; having or producing antibodies or lymphocytes capable of reacting with a specific antigen. It is my belief that in our ultimate purpose, God makes us immune to the people we are supposed to help. Really think about that for a minute. Let's take getting a flu vaccination for instance. Every year, like clockwork, many of us visit our family physician, pharmacy, clinics or local community health centers to get an annual flu vaccine. These vaccinations protect us against infection from influenza viruses. The interesting thing about the vaccination is it actually is made with the flu virus. That's right! The flu virus (inactivated) is part of the vaccine that protects us from the flu.

Let's put that in context as it relates to purpose. You survived something that others haven't and, if it happened to you, it's happened or is happening to someone else. Just like the doctor administers the flu shot to prevent you from getting the flu, is the same way God allows us to encounter things in life to strengthen us and help us build up a resistance to those very things so that when we come in contact with others who have had similar experiences we can help them without being infected. When you understand this and you take the time to heal from your own past hurts and traumatic experiences, you now become the "cure", for someone else with the same "disease".

God uses our natural gifts, the ones that make room for us, to find the people we are supposed to impact. That's the only reason for the gifts. He gives us charisma in the area of our gifts and he shines through it. When we are operating in our gifts, we make it look easy and that is especially attractive to others. However, it's very important to know that healing must take place first so that what's attracted to the gifts won't contaminate the vessel or agent. HEALING is a must! The agent is supposed to be the cure for the illness, therefore it can't be tainted or infected in any way. The more you tap into who God made you to be, the greater your impact and effect on others. You become the dose or the vehicle needed to push them into their healing and ultimately into their purpose.

It is so important to recognize and understand the effects your past hurts and traumatic experiences have had on you. These things can have a direct effect on your everyday life. They often shape our perceptions, distort our perceptions, mold our behavior towards others, affects how we interact with people, and causes us to be private and emotionally unavailable. The seeds of our hurts and traumatic experiences grow out and show up in many of these forms. In so many instances we look at the end result or what we see has manifested itself in someone and chalk it up as a character flaw. Instead of labeling them as combative, angry, abrasive, insubordinate, etc., we should be asking, WHY? Why do they come off that way?

This is where true purpose begins! You will know and you'll be able to quickly identify when someone has been through a similar experience by the following:

1. **Natural:** The way the seed grows out or shows up in one's behavior will probably look like me or similar to me (*i.e., reserved, hard exterior, angry, bitter, etc.*)

2. **Spiritual:** Spirits attract like spirits. Your spirit man will recognize the same underlying pain and experiences of others. It will know that this person is in need the same healing and purpose you are now experiencing.

Chapter Three: Heal and Deal

Emotional abuse, physical abuse, abandonment, sexual abuse, verbal and psychological abuse, whatever those things are that have left you hurting, hopeless and broken are the very things you must heal from! Additionally, they are exactly what God wants to use through you to help others.

This healing process will require you to purge out all the bad and refill by becoming an open portal/vessel for your gifting and purpose to flow through. Empty so that you may be filled again, this time with God's love and purpose for your life. This will be one of the most vulnerable places you'll experience. This phase is so necessary for true healing, but it can leave you feeling weak and helpless. Be reminded that His strength is made perfect in your weakness! Keep that before you.

I'm not an expert in healing but I share my story and the lessons I've learned because I have experienced healing in some of the deepest of levels; all because of several principles God used to teach me through my own life experiences. Healing is two-fold and requires two things, an offender and the offended. The offended is quite often referred to as a victim but because we are discussing purpose, I tend to think of the offended person as a "healing predator".

Wake Up! An Awakening of Purpose

I know, I know, the word predator may alarm you a bit and that's okay. I've found that most don't like the word because it is often associated with a negative connotation or meaning behind it. When you hear the word you probably get a vision of tiger devouring its prey in the wild. Or maybe we envision people being exploited or taken advantage of. We often receive the word predator in a negative sense because often, we have been preyed upon or exploited in some way. Of course not by a tiger, but by people who were trying to devour us or take advantage of us for their personal gain. But, what if we could be predators in a positive light. What if we could be on the prowl seeking out those in healing? What if we could ruthlessly expose people to their own healing? What if after being healed ourselves, we could show others how to become the hunter and not the hunted?

What people need is coming from you! You have the cure. You have what they need. When you really put that in perspective you become aware of the urgency and sensitivity. More importantly, you understand you cannot keep the healing that you've been exposed to, to yourself. When you experience true healing you can't keep it to yourself! Purpose is directly connected to your past hurts, traumatic experiences, and poor decisions. Some of which are directly connected to your family.

Healing will require you to first, face the hurt and trauma of your past. Naturally, someone who doesn't know they need to be healed will try to suppress the feeling, emotion or memory. Often putting it on a "shelf" to hopefully, never have to deal with it again. I'm here to tell you, I've tried that and failed epically. It doesn't work. Those "on-the-shelf" experiences will come bubbling up in one form or another.

I was aware that I needed to be healed so I started what I thought was a process of healing. After getting to a certain point, I thought I had done all the internal healing I needed to do. But, unlike every other problem or situation that came against me, I never really addressed the effects of the traumas and hurts of my past head on. The pinned up emotional bile left me so hardened, angry, and agitated; causing me to lash out in some of the most immature and unflattering ways. This was just one of the ways the seed of my hurt manifested itself, often showing up as character flaws, poor decisions, and bad habits.

As someone in the music industry, my work often consists of late nights and long weekends. Monday's are typically my "rest" days. It's the time I use to recharge for the remainder of the week. Don't get me wrong, some of my rest time includes lying around, watching television and eating my favorite snacks. Don't judge me. This one particular Monday morning, I was watching the show, Marriage Boot-Camp; Reality Stars - Hip Hop Edition on WeTV (again, don't judge me lol). Participants of the show are reality TV couples. Under the guidance of therapists, Dr. Ish and Dr. V, the couples come on the show to put their relationships through a test and work through their relationship issues. Episode seven of Season 12, was entitled *Breaking Bad*. This particular episode was so moving. Using a graffiti wall display to post their experiences, participants were forced to go back to the traumatic pasts of their childhoods.

When the participants began exposing some of the horrific things in their pasts that they had been through, I began to break. I found myself on every wall except one or two. What stuck with me was when I heard the therapist say that entertainers learn to express their pain through their art and that's great, but expression is not confronting and dealing with the issues and experiences. I couldn't tell you what happened after that because I literally broke at that point. Out of the entire episode, that was the very piece I needed to see and hear. It shed light on a hard truth for me, a pill I wasn't ready to swallow. As much as I professed it to myself, I really wasn't healed. In that moment I was so emotional and I had such an array of emotions that I couldn't even articulate it. Like many of you, I thought I was fine but something triggered the very thing I needed to address. I charge you to be aware and understand that when you really want healing, I mean REALLY want it…it just might show up in different forms. Forms that you aren't even expecting. Don't be afraid, instead take full advantage of those moments and deal with the emotions.

Wake Up! An Awakening of Purpose

You may not be an entertainer, but perhaps you have been showing up as someone other than the true you. Maybe you have suppressed and purposely chosen not to deal with your issues and problems; leading you to put on a show to hide who you really are and what you really need. Acknowledge what you are feeling and dig into the process of why you are feeling that way. We have to want to rid ourselves of these toxins that are eating us up. We are on borrowed time so time is of the essence. You are an agent with a mission. You have no time to waste!

In relation to addiction, the first thing an addict must do is acknowledge the fact that they have a problem. Next, the addict must take the necessary action to address the problem. How often do we hear people express their lack conviction or care for the consequences or end results of their habits and actions? Then somehow, we allow ourselves to form an opinion of this addict only to make ourselves look like we don't need as much work. Today, I'm here to challenge your perception on healing. Until you heal from what you need to heal from and until you allow your healing create life changes, then it's safe to say we are no different than the drug addict or alcoholic we look down on.

I am blessed to have some of the most powerful, praying, kingdom minded friends and mentors. While praying with one of those friend's one night, I recall being so fed up and just tired. I kept asking, "What is all of this for? All I felt was this pain and I didn't know what to do with it." I just knew that I no longer wanted to feel that pain and agony and the first thing I had to do is not be addicted any longer. It's a very difficult process to kick a habit. We tend to walk around with this baggage and pinned up emotions like bad habits. After practicing a bad habit for years, it can take just as long if not longer to kick it. Think about that and be fair to yourself. Allow yourself the process and the time of kicking your bad emotional habits and character flaws or what I like to refer to as *purpose wounds*.

Once you've acknowledged that you are in need of healing, then it's time to be real. I'm sure those things that happened to you weren't warranted, they probably weren't fair and more than likely, there should have been consequences for the actions of the ones who have offended you. What makes it worse is most of the time the offenders are those closest to you. But what I have learned is the enemy does his best work through SILENCE. Because people can be very emotional and irrational we tend to not want to expose the situation. As hard as it may be, it's imperative to your healing. Open up to a trusted source and expose the devil's device of silence!

Breaking the silence requires a strategy. I used what I refer to as the "steak strategy". You read correctly, this process is similar to how you would cook a raw piece of steak. Just as any uncooked food, there are steps necessary to properly prepare the food for cooking. With steak, there are three basic steps you want to take; clean it, tenderize it, and season it! For the sake of explaining this process, let's think of the offender's heart as that steak.

Cleaning

This is where you check your motives at the door. We already know that emotions may be high but compose yourself. Any specialty knockout boxer will tell you, sometimes you have to take a hit to get the shot you want. Chin up for the greater good of the match! Know that when you are trying to rectify a situation where someone has been offended, more times than none, the original offender will find a way to feel offended! This is more of a dodging technique so they don't have to deal with the weight and responsibility of being wrong and ultimately, having to apologize. This part of the mission will be tough, but it's necessary for healing.

As tough as it may be, put yourself in the offender's shoes. In any relationship, it takes two to make it work. YOU ARE NOT PERFECT! Just as you will need grace and compassion when you slip (and you will), you will have to extend it first. Apologize (genuinely) for anything you may have done that has offended the offender. This wipes the slate clean for you and allows some of the walls between you and the offender to start to crumble.

Always check your motives and remain in the offender's shoes when reconciling. It's important that you NEVER leave from that position while you are apologizing and speaking. This helps keep your ego in check and allows you to express from a place of compassion and

empathy rather than a place of accusation. Your mission here is not to get an apology. The goal is to experience true healing and that comes from within. The truth is it's our pride that wants to hear an apology. However, because the offender will be taken aback by your stance and the walls have started to be torn down, they will often soften up, acknowledge the offense and then offer an apology. If they don't, that is okay too. Let them deal with that part. This is about you experiencing the true healing you need.

Tenderizing

This process starts with the confronting stage. This phase isn't about pointing fingers or blaming the offender, but rather about you expressing to this person that their forgiveness is essential for your healing and the ability to freely move on with your life.

Seasoning

Express how you don't want the tension and if possible, you want a healthy relationship. Not one resembling the dysfunction of the past! After all of this is done, the healing process has begun and has taken root. It's important to note, there is no time limit on how long your process may take. For some it may take weeks, for other months or even years. If I knew what I know now back then I would tell my younger self to take pleasure in the process because that's where real character comes from.

Now if you're like me you're probably saying "Okay, what about me? THE REAL OFFENDED ONE". I'm so glad you asked. So here's the thing...if the offender didn't apologize before or after the conversation, then chances are they may never apologize. Tough I know, but let that on their conscious not yours. It's on them! That should offer an even greater sense of release for you. Now let's deal with it. When we help others heal we ignite our healing process even more. You will feel less of a victim and less offended. This is good because being a healing agent requires a heart and posture of compassion. Although the offender should be doing the work to make it right, the fact is you just might have to be the one to get the process going. You may have to be the initiator in this process. Like me, you may have tried to get help but it didn't work. It wasn't effective. The help I was getting didn't have any impact on me healing, so it wasn't working.

I grew up in church and that's all I had was "church". Aside from providing for my family it didn't hold any stock in my decision making. Nothing worked and nothing would work until I was ready for the process of losing those things I felt made me who I was. I was partially right, but I had it backwards. I thought the pain I felt from my past made me "real", more authentic than others. It made me feel genuine and raw because I saw so many people living lives that were all lies. So, in my mind, at least I was "real"! I felt like I had EVERY right to say ANYTHING, and whatever I said I meant it. "I say what I mean and I mean what I say because life made me that way" became my stance. All the while, I had it all backwards. I thought my pain made me and because of my warped perception, I hurt a lot of amazing people along the way. Those deeply planted seeds grew out to be very ugly because there had been too much silence and too much time -- but I got it JUST in time and so will you! I've come to learn that the things I went through and survived, made me who I am today. They have equipped me with everything I need for the new purposed life as an agent of healing.

The main objective for this whole mission is for you to heal from your past. When exposed to or see those areas of trauma, after you have been healed, those things can no longer affect you. I'm sure you have heard the saying "play the hand you're dealt". This same saying applies even as it pertains to your individual purpose. When people are in you your metron or circle of influence, you have the ability and responsibility to recognize the very signs of pain and hurts you have now healed from. Not only to recognize them but to help lead others to begin their own journey of healing.

Chapter Four: Spiritual Maintenance

There's an idea out here that the less transgression you commit the more spiritual you are. Lies!!!! Your flesh and your spirit are two different entities. Although one may affect the other, they require their own attention. Having discipline and being wise in judgment helps you handle the flesh. However, just because you have your priorities in order, you're not reckless in your decision making, you are financially responsible and you don't put yourself in troubling, irresponsible and risky situations; it doesn't mean you are more spiritually aware. Your spirit is very delicate and you must handle it with care! It's your spirit that can take you places your gifting can't. It can break barriers and generational curses. It can unlock things you'll need for the rest of your walk in purpose!

Awareness of your spirit man is imperative to operating and fulfilling your purpose. The Word of God says in 1 Corinthians 2:14, "But the natural man receiveth not the things of the Spirit of God: for they are foolishness unto him: neither can he know them, because they are spiritually discerned." What this scripture is saying is that God illuminates our spirit in order to teach us the things of God. You cannot receive that in the natural. I watched a video some time ago that gave me a better understanding of this. Before watching the video, I used to think that tapping into one's spirit was some mystical thing that only happened to special people. However, the presenter in the video explained the spirit man in such a way that was so practical.

What I now understand is because we are special people who are merely spirits wrapped in flesh, we have the power to tap into our spirit man and see, speak and hear without using our natural senses. When you allow the Spirit of God to activate your spirit and you actually tap into that, your spirit puts you in another dimension. Making you more spiritually aware than you could have ever imagined. We are agents from another dimension! God put you in a body and gave you a specific mission and purpose. Begin seeing, hearing and speaking in the spirit in order to carry out the mission you have been given. Just like anything else, the more you put this into practice the stronger you will become, the stronger you spirit man will become and the easier it will be. The more aware you are of your spiritual being the more you will operate in it. Your mission, ultimately, is to help the very individuals that are much like yourself; wandering the earth lost with no clear sense of direction, no awareness of self and an undiscovered purpose!

Before going through my own extensive healing process, I used to see myself through the hurts, pains and disappointments of life, going all the way back to childhood. Not only was that unhealthy, but it's exactly where the enemy wanted me. Not until I had an encounter with one of my very own real life angels, did that begin to change. Although she was a woman of few words, she spoke to my spirit! She spoke life over my entire future saying, "Your spirit needs to be felt around the world. You can sing, but it's your spirit that will attract people to you". That day, I was even more intrigued because I wanted to see what she saw in my spirit!

That conversation coupled with God's love, healing and grace, confirmed to me, I am not what I endured! And guess what? Neither are you! You are not what you endured! The abuse, the abandonment, the mistreatment; you are none of those things that you faced. What those things are however, are the direct link to your purpose and those you are called to. So, take the time to reflect on the things you want to forget or block out. They are the very things that have made you strong, ready, potent, and necessary to the world.

Chapter Five: Finding the Real Me

A vital step after your healing process is to identify how those pains and traumas of your past have manifested in your life. How has it shown up in your perception, character flaws, attitudes, actions or emotions? Before delving into this, know whatever pain or disappointments happened to you in your life was not your fault. As painful and hurtful as it was, it shaped you and built you into the special person you are.

Be careful not to allow guilt to overtake you. Guilt will cause you to settle for things you really don't want or need, because you feel undeserving. This can hinder us when it comes to really being effective and healthy as it pertains to you being completely free in being you. There were so many times, I allowed things to happen to me or around me when I knew I could have easily corrected it with a simple conversation, or a simple no. But out of guilt, I'd often end up getting the brunt end of the stick. Which usually ended with me being pissed because deep down inside, I knew better. When I started forgiving others, I would often forget to forgive the most important person…myself.

In this next phase of your life, you have to be free in your truth! Although people can interpret your truth the way they choose to, they can't take away or alter YOUR TRUTH! When you are free in yourself, no one can ever use your own mistakes or downfalls against you. Those things I was afraid to face have become the best arsenal I've ever had! They are my tools that I have to pull out occasionally to help someone else through their situations and healing. You never know who needs to just hear your story, MISTAKES INCLUDED! This alone may free others.

Purpose requires you to use everything you wanted to forget, especially the mistakes. I like to call mistakes "purpose lessons" because you'll need all of those lessons in order to fulfil purpose. Over time you will see that all things really do work together for your good according to the Big Boss' purpose. Release the guilt! When the guilt is gone, you can really start to change some things. True change and evolution is a choice. Guilt keeps us defensive and always making excuses like, "I've been this way for years". Losing the guilt says, this is how I was, but now I'm growing and evolving. It acknowledges that you understand this behavior, emotion or thought process has to change and that you were this way because of life, BUT NOW it's time to take control over your life and wake up to true purpose! As you grow and evolve, once you identify an issue that gets in the way of your purpose and true happiness, you will want to do what you need to in order to change that.

Naturally as you get older, your vision may start to get worse. You know, when objects are distorted and you can't see things as clearly as you used to so you start squinting. When this happens we simply go to an optometrist and get corrective lenses. The optometrist is skilled and knows which tests to run in order to identify exactly what prescription strength we will need. Like an optometrist, we have an amazing doctor who knows just what we need. In turn, he strategically sends individuals in our lives to be those corrective lenses, helping us to focus and see clearer. Though not always comfortable, it's important to have people you love and trust to be able to correct you. It's even more important that you are open to the correction.

Chapter Six: The Mind Game

The mind is amazing yet complex at the same time. We often must remind ourselves to start afresh each day. You will have to practice a certain level of discipline and train yourself to compete with the mind every single day! The mind is comprised of memories, imaginations and intellect. Let's define each of those terms according to Merriam-Webster.

- *Memory* is the power or process of reproducing or recalling what has been learned and retained especially through associative mechanisms. The store of things learned and retained from an organism's activity or experience as evidenced by modification of structure or behavior or by recall and recognition

- *Imagination* is the act or power of forming a mental image of something not present to the senses or never before wholly perceived in reality: creative ability: ability to confront and deal with a problem.

- *Intellect* is the power of knowing as distinguished from the power to feel and to will: the capacity for knowledge. The capacity for rational or intelligent thought especially when highly developed

Rules to the Game: You versus the Mind

Every morning you have to make a conscious effort to filter through memories, imaginations and intellect before you even start your day. If your mind recalls a situation as being a bad one, make yourself see how it worked out or is working out in your favor. Imagine yourself overcoming those things instead of being overtaken by them. The mind is so powerful that you can will yourself to wellness and healing simply by imagining it. Once your imagination is charged with this amazing picture of you whole, your intellect then kicks in. By information and intelligence, your intellect will attempt to contradict what you are imagining. Train your mind! Reprogram what you know. How do you do that? I'm glad you asked. Saturate your mind with the good things; things that pertain to your healed, healthy, whole, new self. This way even if an old memory or imagination resurfaces, your reprogrammed intellect will reel you back in. For your own mental health, you have to work on all three of these factors. Be consistent and deliberate about it. When you get up in the morning, throughout your day and before you retire to bed at night, affirm who you are and what you will accomplish.

Learning new things about yourself will be necessary as you walk in this new found truth! It may be hard at first to remain conscious of these things but like anything we have to learn, when we are consistent it becomes a habit. Good habits form when the mind works with you and not against you. When you change your perceptions on life and how you see yourself, you actually shift the trajectory of your life.

The devil tries to set up camp in our minds to keep us from knowing who we are in God and keep us from our purpose. The enemy is just a squatter living in the minds of people who are sleep to their purpose. In the natural, when squatters have set up shop and begin living in someone else's home, there is a process to get them out. Even though they are there illegally, there is still a legal process that has to happen to evict them. Can you believe that? Different from the other saying, my saying is *"A sleep mind is the devils workshop, but a woke mind is the devils kryptonite"*. The enemy's job is to alter your perception and pollute your thoughts. When that doesn't work he will send distractions your way to knock your focus off. Understand that this is a battle in itself and though you may get knocked down occasionally, you will get back up. This will only happen when you are intentional about renewing your mind daily. Be conscious of the power of your mind. Now that you are awake, STAY WOKE!

Fear is the Real Op (Opponent)

You may be a little apprehensive about this new way of living, learning, thinking, and evolving. As liberating as it is, there might be some hesitation about being who you are truly called to be on this earth. Do you recognize that which is trying to creep in? It's called FEAR. Fear paralyzes you and it will have you doing some of the craziest things ever. Crazy like seeing a person riding a bike, and then a dog starts to chase them. Instead of them just pedaling a little faster, they jump off and run! How crazy is that? That is exactly what fear does if we let that emotion drive us. It causes us to be irrational and haste in our decisions. Fear is merely an illusion and it's one of the enemy's greatest devices. You have control over fear and any illusions when we reprogram our imagination! Through our intellect we understand that we have absolutely no reason to fear anyone or anything! For we are made in God's image with His Spirit. God's Spirit doesn't know fear! God's Spirit knows love, power and a sound mind! So, that's what we must know.

Chapter Seven: Love and Passions

Life often programs to think that the things we love the most have to be put on the back burner for the sake of reality. As children we are encouraged to let out imaginations run wild and put on our "creative hats". All the while we discouraged from those things in our adulthood because they tend to bring little stability. So what do we do? We ignore them. We sit on the very gifts, dreams and things we are passionate about to settle for jobs that will keep us stable. We stay on these jobs unhappy, constantly undervalued, and more often than none, over worked and under paid.

I challenge you after going through your healing and becoming this new, spiritually aware, available, mind transformed and ready-to-go agent, go back to when you were a child. Recall those gifts and talents you sat to the side and go back and pick them up. Match them with the visions and dreams God gave you, then get to work! This is so important in order to be able to have a consistent posture of love! There is a familiar parable in the bible about talents *(see below).*

Matthew 25:14–30 tells of a master who was leaving his house to travel, and, before leaving, entrusted his property to his servants. According to the abilities of each man, one servant received five talents, the second servant received two talents, and the third servant received one talent. The property entrusted to the three servants was worth 8 talents, where a talent was a significant amount of money. Upon returning home, after a long absence, the master asks his three servants for an account of the talents he entrusted to them. The first and the second servants explain that they each put their talents to work, and have doubled the value of the property with which they were entrusted; each servant was rewarded:

His master said to him, 'Well done, good and faithful servant. You have been faithful over a little; I will set you over much. Enter into the joy of your master.'

Matthew 25:23, New English Translation

The third servant, however, had merely hidden his talent, had buried it in the ground, and was punished by his master:

Then the one who had received the one talent came and said, 'Sir, I knew that you were a hard man, harvesting where you did not sow, and gathering where you did not scatter seed, so I was afraid, and I went and hid your talent in the ground. See, you have what is yours.' But his master answered, 'Evil and lazy servant! So you knew that I harvest where I didn't sow and gather where I didn't scatter? Then you should have deposited my money with the bankers, and on my return I would have received my money back with interest! Therefore take the talent from him and give it to the one who has ten. For the one who has will be given more, and he will have more than enough. But the one who does not have, even what he has will be taken from him. And throw that worthless slave into the outer darkness, where there will be weeping and gnashing of teeth.'

Wake Up! An Awakening of Purpose

This parable ignited a fire under me and I would work hard to gain value from others. I wanted a pat on the back for how good I was but the reality was that I was merely a pawn in someone else's operation. The whole time neglecting the empire (hiding talents) within myself. I started embracing all the gifts and talents I had been sitting on, which in turn, they brought me more VALUE than I had ever gained working for someone else's company or organization. You too have amazing gifts and talents inside of you that will really add value to your life! If you faithfully devote even a portion of the time you commit to your 40 hour work-week to your talents and gifts you would be amazed at the level of peace and happiness you will have. This takes a level of awareness and faith that only the Creator who has given you the gifts and talents can give. Inside of you is all of the value and worth you have been seeking through affirmation and acceptance from others.

By watching others utilize their gifts and talents responsibly, I came to the realization that I have to get up off of my butt and get to work! I have gifts, talents and a story to inspire the world, so what was I waiting for? I wasted a lot of time seeking validation from others when all the while, the value is in me. I started operating out of pure love and passion for my purpose and it's my new normal. It's become my way of living. Love first. When you reach purpose and you filter your gifts through passion and love, it makes your spirit attractive. Your motives have to be pure at this point.

Wake Up! An Awakening of Purpose

You don't want to go back to the bad habits, never ending cycles and guilt that you have been freed from.

Love always wins. True love will find you while you are working in purpose. Why, you ask? Because purpose needs a partner! You'll find that everything you need to help your purpose, is often right in front of you. You just have to know who they are. We can entertain angels unknowingly and because we don't know or recognize them, we often mishandle them. Usually, because they don't look the way we want or the way we expect them to. Don't be closed to the possibility of your enemies being that blessing to you. Your enemies are not only expected but essential in pushing you to purpose. The ones that have talked about you and hurt you, will be the very ones that need what you have inside of you the most! This next phase of your life will be one for the books. Don't be surprised when you are experiencing some of the best relationships, friendships, memories while living out your dreams. Be WHOLE. Be AWARE. Be OPEN. Be AWAKENED. You are an agent obligated to go complete every assignment God sends your way! We are in this world but not of it, so don't be afraid to go back and find those things the world needs from you. Whatever you do, do it with love and love doing it! Your gifts and talents are great but know, behind every talent is a compelling story and testimony. The world needs both!

Awakening Exercises

As mentioned in my introduction, I am not a counselor nor a spiritual advisor. However, I have included some of the exercises that I have used in my own healing and awakening process in hopes that they will help you in your own awakening. These exercises are not the end all be all. They are merely a way to start the process. I encourage you to seek professional counseling and therapy to discuss and further explore your responses. Now let's get started!

Awakening Exercise #1

What are some of the areas of your life where you have been sleeping, in a state of unawareness or need to be awakened?

Awakening Exercise #2

How have past hurts, traumatic situations or bad decisions contributed to you "sleeping" through life?

Awakening Exercise #3

Letter Written but Unsent: Write a letter to the offender, the person, situation, or decision that has caused pain in your life. Once completed, DESTROY the letter. This exercise is more about you releasing those bottled up thoughts and feelings. You may need to write several and that's okay too.

Awakening Exercise #4

Affirmations are important in your healing. For many of us, we need to awaken our spirits by reinforcing the positive thoughts of who we are! You can do this by training your spirit to know through affirmations. Affirmations will encourage your spirit and reestablish a new found confidence in the real you!

I encourage you to say your affirmations silently then aloud. Silently affirms your spirit, aloud trains your mind. Take the time to write several affirmations that you will recite daily. Begin each affirmation with I am…

My Daily Affirmations

Example:

I AM <u>worthy of everything God has for me!</u>

I AM _____

I AM _____

I AM _____

I AM _____

I AM _____

I AM _____

I AM _____

I AM _____

I AM _____

I AM _____

I AM _____

I AM _____

I AM _____

I AM _____

I AM _____

Awakening Exercise #5

After finishing this book, what steps will you take to wake up and awaken your purpose?

Bibliography

Parable of the talents or minas. (n.d.). In Wikipedia. Retrieved April 14, 2019, from https://en.wikipedia.org/wiki/Parable_of_the_talents_or_minas

Definitions (n.d.). In Merriem-Webster. Retrieved April 25, 2019, from https://www.merriam-webster.com/

Acknowledgments

I would like to extend a special thank you to my parents, spiritual leaders, mentors and friends who have supported and helped me along the way. Your continued support and encouragement means the world to me.

Blessings to you all and thanks again!

About the Author

Jermaine Holland (J. Holland), owner of Mind of Music, is an author, emerging singer-songwriter and producer whose musical roots run deep.

Growing up in a musical family, Jermaine began playing the piano at nine years old. Playing piano only peaked Jermaine's musical interests and pursuits. Eventually, leading him to discover his gift of singing. Jermaine has since expanded his musical career not only as a vocalist and musician, but as a songwriter, vocal arranger, producer, consultant, entrepreneur, vocal coach and mentor.

Jermaine's love and passion for music is evident to everyone he meets. He pours his heart and soul into each project he's a part of. Jermaine not only delivers excellence, he expects it! He is no stranger to hard work. Jermaine works tirelessly perfecting his craft, often putting in long hours in studio sessions, rehearsals and performances.

Jermaine is selfless and has a heart to help others. He often mentors new artists and musicians; sharing what he has learned throughout his life and music career. Jermaine has a way of connecting with people. His authenticity and straightforwardness is refreshing for many. Jermaine uses every opportunity to pour into the lives of others, especially when it comes to them finding their purpose.

A self-proclaimed Purpose Finder, Jermaine knows what it is to embrace each day with anticipation and excitement knowing you are operating in purpose.

Made in the USA
Middletown, DE
10 June 2019